Meditations with
Teilhard de Chardin

Meditations With

Teilhard de Chardin

Introduction
and Versions by
Blanche Marie Gallagher, B.V.M.

Foreword by
Jean Houston

BEAR & COMPANY
SANTA FE, NEW MEXICO

Library of Congress Cataloging-in-Publication Data
Teilhard de Chardin, Pierre.
    Meditations with Teilhard de Chardin.
Bibliography: p.
    1. Meditations. I. Gallagher, Blanche Marie,
1922-   . II. Title.
BX2182.2.T37 1988   242   88-10536
ISBN 0-939680-47-5 (pbk.)

Bear & Company
P.O. Drawer 2860
Santa Fe, NM 87504

Design: Kathleen Katz
Illustration: Blanche Gallagher
Typography: Casa Sin Nombre, Ltd.
Printed in the United States of America by BookCrafters.

9 8 7 6 5 4 3 2 1

Contents

Foreword

One of the greatest privileges of my life was the opportunity of knowing a man given to human wonder and divine seizure who was in turn so loving of everyone and everything whom he saw or met that the universe turned a corner for those of us fortunate enough to be in his presence. His was truly the Christic journey and his path was strewed with many miracles of love made manifest. Let me tell you what being with him was like. Let me tell you about walking the dog with Teilhard De Chardin, or Mr. Tayer as I called him then.*

When I was about fourteen, I used to run down Park Avenue in New York City, late for high school. I was a great big overgrown girl (5 feet eleven by the age of eleven) and one day I ran into a rather frail old gentleman in his seventies and knocked the wind out of him. He laughed as I helped him to his feet and asked me in French-accented speech, "Are you planning to run like that for the rest of your life?"

"Yes, sir," I replied. "It looks that way."

"Well, Bon Voyage!" he said.

"Bon Voyage!" I answered and sped on my way.

About a week later I was walking down Park Avenue with my fox terrier, Champ, and again I met the old gentleman.

"Ah," he greeted me, "my friend the runner, and with a fox terrier. I knew one like that years ago in France. Where are you going?"

"Well, sir," I replied, "I'm taking Champ to Central Park."

"I will go with you," he informed me. "I will take my constitutional."

And thereafter, for about a year or so, the old gentleman and I would meet and walk together often several times a week in Central Park. He had a long French name but asked me to call him by the first part of it, which was "Mr. Tayer," as far as I could make out.

The walks were magical and full of delight. Not only did Mr. Tayer seem to have absolutely no self-consciousness, but he was always being seized by wonder and astonishment over the simplest things. He was constantly and literally falling into love. I remember one time when he suddenly fell on his knees, his long Gallic nose raking the ground, and exclaimed to me, "Jeanne, look at the caterpillar. Ahhhh!" I joined him on the ground to see what had evoked so profound a response that he was seized by the essence of caterpillar. "How beautiful it is," he remarked, "this little green being with its wonderful funny little feet. Exquisite! Little furry body, little green feet on the road to metamorphosis." He then regarded me with equal delight. "Jeanne, can you feel yourself to be a caterpillar?"

"Oh yes," I replied with the baleful knowing of a gangly, pimply faced teenager.

"Then think of your own metamorphosis," he suggested. "What will you be when you become a butterfly, *une papillon*, eh? What is the butterfly of Jeanne?" (What a great question for a fourteen-year-old girl!) His long, gothic, comic-tragic face would nod with wonder. "Eh, Jeanne, look at the clouds! God's calligraphy in the sky! All that transforming, moving, changing, dissolving, becoming. Jeanne, become a cloud and become all the forms that ever were."

Or there was the time that Mr. Tayer and I leaned into the strong wind that suddenly whipped through Central Park, and he told me, "Jeanne, sniff the wind." I joined him in taking great snorts of wind. "The same wind may once have been sniffed by Jesus Christ (sniff), by Alexander the Great (sniff), by Napoleon (sniff), by Voltaire (sniff), by Marie Antoinette (sniff)!" (There seemed to be a lot of French people in that wind.) "Now sniff this next gust of wind in very deeply for it contains. . . *Jeanne d'Arc*! Sniff the wind once sniffed by Jeanne d'Arc. Be filled with the winds of history."

It was wonderful. People of all ages followed us around,

laughing—not at us but with us. Old Mr. Tayer was truly diaphanous to every moment and being with him was like being in attendance at God's own party, a continuous celebration of life and its mysteries. But mostly Mr. Tayer was so full of vital sap and juice that he seemed to flow with everything. Always he saw the interconnections between things—the way that everything in the universe, from fox terriers to tree bark to somebody's red hat to the mind of God, was related to everything else and was very, very good. He wasn't merely a great appreciator, engaged by all his senses. He was truly penetrated by the reality that was yearning for him as much as he was yearning for it. He talked to the trees, to the wind, to the rocks as dear friends, as beloved even. "Ah, my friend, the mica schist layer, do you remember when . . . ?" And I would swear that the mica schist would begin to glitter back. I mean, mica schist will do that, but on a cloudy day?! Everything was treated as personal, as sentient, as "thou." And everything that was thou was ensouled with being, and it thou-ed back to him. So when I walked with him, I felt as though a spotlight was following us, bringing radiance and light everywhere. And I was constantly seized by astonishment in the presence of this infinitely beautiful man, who radiated such sweetness, such kindness.

I remember one occasion when he was quietly watching a very old woman watching a young boy play a game. "Madame," he suddenly addressed her. She looked up, surprised that a stranger in Central Park would speak to her. "Madame," he repeated, "why are you so fascinated by what that little boy is doing?" The old woman was startled by the question, but the kindly face of Mr. Tayer seemed to allay her fears and evoke her memories. "Well, sir," she replied in an ancient but pensive voice, "the game that boy is playing is like one I played in this park around 1880, only it's a mite different." We noticed that the boy was listening, so Mr. Tayer promptly included him in the conversation. "Young fellow, would you like to learn the game as it was played so many years ago?"

"Well...yeah, sure, why not?" the boy replied. And soon the young boy and the old woman were making friends and sharing old and new variations on the game—as unlikely an incident to occur in Central Park as could be imagined.

But perhaps the most extraordinary thing about Mr. Tayer was the way that he would suddenly look at you. He looked at you with wonder and astonishment joined to unconditional love joined to a whimsical regarding of you as the cluttered house that hides the holy one. I felt myself primed to the depths by such seeing. I felt evolutionary forces wake up in me by such seeing, every cell and thought and potential palpably changed. I was yeasted, greened, awakened by such seeing, and the defeats and denigrations of adolescence redeemed. I would go home and tell my mother, who was a little skeptical about my walking with an old man in the park so often, "Mother, I was with my old man again, and when I am with him, I leave my littleness behind." That deeply moved her. You could not be stuck in littleness and be in the radiant field of Mr. Tayer.

The last time that I ever saw him was the Thursday before Easter Sunday, 1955. I brought him the shell of a snail. "Ah, escargot," he exclaimed and then proceeded to wax ecstatic for the better part of an hour. Snail shells, and galaxies, and the convolutions in the brain, the whorl of flowers and the meanderings of rivers were taken up into a great hymn to the spiralling evolution of spirit and matter. When he had finished, his voice dropped, and he whispered almost in prayer, "Omega...omega...omega..." Finally he looked up and said to me quietly, "Au revoir, Jeanne."

"Au revoir, Mr. Tayer," I replied, "I'll meet you at the same time next Tuesday."

For some reason, Champ, my fox terrier didn't want to budge, and when I pulled him along, he whimpered, looking back at Mr. Tayer, his tail between his legs. The following Tuesday I was there waiting where we always met at the corner of Park Avenue and 83rd Street. He didn't come. The following Thursday I waited again. Still he didn't come. The dog looked up at me sadly. For the next eight weeks I continued to wait, but he never came again. It turned out that he had suddenly died that Easter Sunday but I didn't find that out for years.

Some years later, someone handed me a book without a cover which was titled *The Phenomenon of Man*. As I read the book I found it strangely familiar in its concepts. Occasional words and expressions loomed up as echoes from my past. When, later in the book, I came across the concept of the "Omega point," I was certain. I asked to see the jacket of the book, looked at the author's picture, and, of course, recognized him immediately. There was no forgetting or mistaking that face. Mr. Tayer was Teilhard de Chardin, the great priest-scientist, poet and mystic, and during that lovely and luminous year I had been meeting him outside the Jesuit rectory of St. Ignatius, where he was living most of the time.

I have often wondered if it was my simplicity and innocence that allowed the fullness of Teilhard's being to be revealed. To me he was never the great priest-paleontologist Pere Teilhard. He was old Mr. Tayer. Why did he always come and walk with me every Tuesday and Thursday, even though I'm sure he had better things to do? Was it that in seeing me so completely he himself could be completely seen at a time when his writings, his work, were proscribed by the Church, when he was not permitted to teach, or even to talk about his ideas? As I later found out, he was undergoing at that time the most excruciating agony that there is—the agony of utter disempowerment and psychological crucifixion. And yet to me he was always so present—whimsical, engaging, empowering. How could that be? I think it was because Teilhard had what few Church officials did—the power and grace of the Love that passes all understanding. He could write about love being the evolutionary force, the Omega point, that lures the world and ourselves into becoming, because he experienced that love in a piece of rock, in the wag of a dog's tail, in the eyes of a child. He was so in love with everything that he talked in great particularity, even to me as an adolescent, about the desire atoms

§ 11 §

have for each other, the yearning of molecules, of organisms, of bodies, of planets, of galaxies, all of creation longing for that radiant bonding, for joining, for the deepening of their condition, for becoming more by virtue of yearning for and finding the other. He knew about the search for the Beloved. His model was Christ. For Teilhard de Chardin, Christ was the Beloved of the soul.

Not long ago I watched a religious sister paint with passion that very lure of becoming. As her brush dipped and weaved, it was as if old "Mr. Tayer" was back again, his sparkling words, his vast enthusiasm, his hymns to creation captured in the evolutionary spirals she was portraying. Her cascade of colors sang the fire of his mind more clearly than any conference of "Teilhardian" scholars. Her images dropped godseeds onto canvas and demanded that we attend to their development in a way that the old man would have mightily applauded.

I know that artist. Her name is Sr. Blanche Marie Gallagher. She and Teilhard would have liked each other very much. And so with the reader's kind permission, may I set up an introduction?

Sister Blanche, I would like to introduce to you my old friend, Father Teilhard. You are kindred souls. The same sparkle seems to shine in your eyes, the same ready laugh and whimsical humor, even the same wash of the tragic sense of things that quickly passes across your faces. You have both roamed the earth to its furthest reaches, he seeking the sacred in the earth, you seeking the sacred in art, both finding that spirit is *mattering* everywhere. You are both master teachers, bringing your students to the shock of recognition as to who and what they really are. You are both midwives of souls. Like potent force fields, you both carry the charge that illumines the minds and hearts of those you meet, that brings the Pattern that Connects and the Possibility that Empowers. And most importantly, you are both so deeply, so passionately committed to the Beloved of the Soul, that your journey is the same one.

Sister Blanche, I think you should write a book of meditations introducing Teilhard's words, and providing some drawings

that express the pith of the man, while letting him express you.
Yes, that is what you should do.

JEAN HOUSTON
Pomona, New York
March, 1988

Jean Houston is internationally known for her work in the field of human development. She is the author of *Life Force: The Psycho-Historical Recovery of the Self, The Possible Human, The Search for the Beloved: Journeys in Sacred Psychology, Godseed: The Journey of Christ,* and the co-author of many other books.

*This story is reprinted from *Godseed: The Journey of Christ,* copyright 1988 by Jean Houston, with permission of Amity House Inc., Warwick, NY 10990.

Preface

My discovery of creation spirituality came as pure gift from the writings of Pierre Teilhard de Chardin. I began studying Teilhard in the late fifties as I searched for a theology of hope. My earlier research as a painter had led me to the art and spiritualities of India, China and Japan. Then I plunged into Teilhard's works to share this scientist-philosopher-poet-priest's experience of the East.

Teilhard did not offer insights into the art and spiritualities of Asia, but his evolutionary creation spirituality presented me with a theological aesthetic. I began viewing nature and my own life through the lens of complexity-consciousness which he constructed for me.

As I continued to reflect upon Teilhard's writings, I found myself drawing on the margins of the books. He startled me into a new awareness of the universe; the material of the Earth came alive for me as cosmic energy.

I pondered his definition of the "biosphere," the matter of the planet incapable of reflective thought. I discovered great inspiration in his concept of the "noosphere," the thinking envelope of the planet made up of the fused creative and intellectual process of each individual on Earth. For Teilhard, the galaxies become a metaphor for this phenomenon of noosphere. Each person's creative-intellectual activity, these "myriad grains of thought," combines with the others of the planet. All this energy unites into constellations of energy by which the universe is brought to its ultimate fulfillment.

I began to paint galaxies. I grew in awareness of the unity within our creative, intellectual and spiritual search. And I realized the tremendous importance of cross-cultural participation in this noosphere.

In this collection of Teilhard's words, I relate to him as a poet—a poet of the universe. These meditations are admittedly selected with personal bias. If one teaches what one needs to learn, I suspect that one writes what one needs to hear.

I have imposed onto Teilhard's writing the structure familiar to students of creation spirituality—the structure of the four paths. I have included the titles of the essays and their dates in the references because the dates provide a sense of the stunning originality of this evolutionary thinker.

Teilhard was not a systematic writer. He wrote in the most unlikely places: in a trench at the front during World War I, in a tent deep in the deserts of China, or while riding on the back of a donkey in Egypt. He also wrote under great psychological stress, for the Roman Catholic church forbad him to publish. But Teilhard fought in defense of his ideas.

His faith and vision have inspired, sustained, and stretched me. I have used this great man's mind to feed my own craft as a painter, teacher, and writer, and to nourish the genesis of my own soul. In these pages, it is my delight to share Teilhard's lavish trust in the creative process, and his challenging hope toward the future.

I dedicate this work to Hank, Dave, Matt, Michael, Robert, Jean, Charlie, and to the members of my religious congregation who have supported my long engagement with Teilhard. I also wish to thank Alice Ryerson Hayes and the Ragdale Foundation for offering me a beautiful haven of peace in which to work on the illustrations.

BLANCHE MARIE GALLAGHER, B.V.M.

1.

Origins:

Nutritious Energies of the Earth

Introduction

I relate to Teilhard as paleontologist, a person who digs deeply into the "nutritious energies of the Earth" not only to recover the past, but, as he insists, to discover the future. Teilhard, the scientist, mines the origins of the planet, and the origins of the race. Eckhart considers the path of savoring and delighting in all of matter as a way of returning to our origins, individually and collectively. Teilhard sought passionately for God in the heart of every substance—this was his form of mysticism, his return to origins.

We find our origins in the heart of matter. And as we tunnel down into the heart of the Earth we arrive at the fireball at the center of our planet, the source of the planet's electromagnetic energy. Pushing through that energy source and back upwards to the crust of the Earth projects us toward the same elemental energy of fire in the sun (Son). The sun for Teilhard forms the warmth of the heart of Christ in the very center of the divine. He posits this flame as the energy of love, "still the most powerful and most unknown energy in the world," which will ultimately lose its contours and become a world aflame.

In a cosmic sense, the world evolves through Matter and Spirit along the direction of two axes. The horizontal axis of Matter pushes toward a higher degree of material complexity and organization. The vertical axis of Spirit evolves toward a higher development of consciousness. And this evolution of Spirit forms a radial energy, the source of interpersonal relationships. The evolution of consciousness creates higher powers of reflection, and ultimately a superconsciousness which Teilhard calls "Omega."

I visualize this as an image of spiraling sun/Son movement generating from God, or the Absolute Evolutionary Force, moving toward the Earth, then meeting a counterspiral which struggles forth from human consciousness toward that ultimate force of pure creativity (see Figure 1: "Origins"). I create from my own center, then seek to share that creative consciousness with others in patterns which radiate through the planet.

Life is art and art is life as it spirals along the path of complexity-consciousness, a parallel to Eckhart's insistence that whatever flows out remains within.

Teilhard expresses his ecological concerns for the "anxieties and desires" of the Earth in 1919. He underscores these anxieties later as the Atomic Age evolves and gives us a renewed need to return to our origins, as well as a fresh need to redefine purity, creativity, and truth.

To understand the world
knowledge is not enough,
you must
 see it,
  touch it,
   live in its presence
and drink the vital heat
of existence in the very heart
 of reality.

In the beginning was *Power*,
     intelligent, loving, energizing.
In the beginning was the *Word*,
     supremely capable of mastering
          and molding
whatever might come into being in the world of matter.
In the beginning there were not
     coldness and darkness:
          there was the Fire.

P*henomenally* speaking,
we see the world
not merely as a system that is simply in movement,
but as one that is in a state of genesis.

The Earth was probably covered by a layer of water
   from which emerged
      the first traces of future continents.
Then those same waters must have begun writhing
   with minute creatures.
      And from that initial proliferation
stemmed the amazing profusion of organic matter
whose matted complexity came to form the last
   (or rather the last but one)
      of the envelopes of our planet:
         the *biosphere*.

Creatures can come into being
like shoots from a stem,
only as part of an endlessly renewed process
of evolution.

That magic word "evolution"
   which haunted my thoughts like a tune:
      which was to me like unsatisfied hunger,
   like a promise held out to me,
   like a summons to be answered.

Evolution assumes its true figure
for our mind and our heart.
It is certainly not "creative,"
as science for a brief moment believed;
but it is the expression of creation,
for our experience,
in time and space.

The operation that creation gives rise to
and that it forms
is infinitely refracted in creatures
in which the work of creation
is materialized and assimilated.

I began to distinguish the arrangement-curve...
not the gentle drift towards equilibrium and rest,
but the irresistible "Vortex" which spins into itself,
    always in the same direction,
        the whole Stuff of things,
from the most simple to the most complex:
spinning it into ever more comprehensive
and more astronomically complicated nuclei.
And the result of this structural torsion
is an increase of consciousness,
        or a rise in psychic temperature.

The consciousness of each of us
is evolution looking at itself
and reflecting upon itself.

Reflection:
the transition which is like a second birth
from simple Life to "Life Squared."

The creative operation of God
does not simply mold us like soft clay.
It is a Fire that animates all it touches,
a spirit that gives life.
So it is *in living*
that we should give ourselves to that creative action,
    imitate it, and
        identify with it.

I give the name of cosmic sense
to the more or less confused affinity
that binds us psychologically to the All
     which envelopes us.
In order that the sense of humanity might emerge,
it was necessary for civilization to begin to encircle
     the Earth.
The cosmic sense
must have been born as soon as humanity found itself
facing the forest, the sea and the stars.
And since then we find evidence of it
in all our experience of the great and unbounded:
     in art,
          in poetry, and
          in religion.

The sense of the Earth
opening and exploding upwards into God;
and the sense of God taking root
and finding nourishment downwards into Earth.

Matter was not ultra-materialized
as I would at first have believed,
but was instead metamorphosed into Psyche.
Spirit was by no means the enemy
on the opposite pole of the Tangibility
which it was seeking to attain:
rather it was its very heart.

Matter and Spirit:
These were no longer two things
but two *states*
or two aspects of one and the same cosmic Stuff,
according to whether it was looked at
or carried further in the direction
    in which it is becoming itself
or in the direction in which it is disintegrating.
        Matter is the Matrix of Spirit.
        Spirit is the higher state of Matter.

Under the irrepressible pressure
of a planet that is contracting upon itself,
we constantly feel, in ourselves
and all around ourselves,
a heightening
of the antagonism between the "tangential" forces
that make us dependent on one another,
and the "radial" aspirations
that urge us towards attaining
    the incommunicable core of our own person.

This is the law of complexity-consciousness,
by which, within life, the Stuff of the cosmos
folds in upon itself continually
    more closely,
following a process of organization,
whose measure is a corresponding increase of tension
    (or psychic temperature).

An ever increasing number of persons
are beginning to distinguish a Noosphere
which is like a halo around the Biosphere.

Noosphere. . .
the living membrane which is stretched like a film
over the lustrous surface of the star
        which holds us.
An ultimate envelope
taking on its own individuality
and gradually detaching itself like a luminous aura
This envelope was not only conscious but thinking. . .
        the Very Soul of the Earth.

The idea is that of the Earth
not only covered by myriads of grains of thought,
     but enclosed in a single thinking envelope
so as to form a single vast grain of thought
on the sidereal scale,
the plurality of individual reflections
grouping themselves together and
    reinforcing one another
      in the act of a single unanimous reflection.

The Noosphere:
The irresistible *setting*
or cementing together of a thinking mass of humans
which is continually more compressed upon itself
by the simultaneous multiplication and expansion
of its individual elements.

Because we are born
and live in the very heart of
this thing that is happening,
we still find it
quite natural not only to think with ourselves
    but also, inevitably,
to think with all other persons at the same time:
in other words, we can't move a finger
without finding ourselves involved in the construction
of a total human act that includes what we see
    and what we make.

Our own age seems primarily to need
a rejuvenation of supernatural forces to be effected
by driving roots deeply into the nutritious energies
of the Earth.
Because it is not
sufficiently moved by a truly human compassion,
because it is not
exalted by a sufficiently passionate admiration
of the universe,
our religion is becoming enfeebled.

For the past century
(and more recently, during the wars)
there have been many points
on which there has been a failure on our part
to understand the anxieties and desires of the Earth:
by not sharing in the great instinctive currents
that control the direction of natural Life,
we have found ourselves
obliged to fall back on the academic counsels
of "human prudence."

In our recent mastery of the Atomic
we have reached the primordial sources
        of the *Energy of Evolution*.
If humankind is to use its new access
of physical power with balanced control,
it cannot do without a rebound of intensity
in its eagerness to act,
        to seek,
                to create.

Purity
is not a debilitating separation
from all created reality,
but an impulse
carrying one through all forms
of created beauty.

Till the very end of time
matter will always remain young,
  exuberant,
    sparkling,
     newborn
       for those who are willing.

It is
in the direction of the fullest
that the truth lies.

2.
Emptying

Introduction

Classical spiritual systems invite us to delight in our common origins, to savor all material realities, and to allow them to bring us to God. They offer us a *via positiva*. But the classical systems also remind us that negative energies confront us as a part of our life on this planet.

Teilhard terms this negative force "entropy": the involution that weighs on us as the heaviness by which our progress is impaired through the dissipation of our creative energy. The pain and suffering encountered in the evolutionary process comes from our lack of unity, and from the plurality, multiplicity and disorganization of our lives and our world.

As we struggle toward inner unity we tend to seek isolation. We attempt to empty our lives of disorganizing energies; we try to "let go." The desire for solitude is a necessary component of all spiritualities, for every creative thought and act proceeds from a centered self. But we are not allowed to remain self enclosed. We find the energies to complete ourselves only by bonding with each other.

Teilhard, an introverted, creative person, finds his energy through solitude. For him, to confront the "other" saps that energy, and the encroachments of others is experienced as suffering. But it is through our common spirit that we bring the noosphere into fulfillment.

Embraced willingly, all suffering carries the potential for progress and fruition on the spiritual path. The mental and physical diminishments we suffer serve a purpose, for the world leaps forward in consciousness when suffering becomes transformed through loving energy.

The weight of entropy tempts us to distortion, disgust, and division. Even when we experience the brief ecstasy of union with God, we return from the encounter with a greater realization of our brokenness. The process of transformation necessitates a downward movement into the vortex of the unconscious (see Figure 2: "Emptying"). The structure of the cross is formed as we grope with the shadow side of the self. However, the cross transfigured becomes a mandala of wholeness when it includes the circle of the sun/Son, the warmth and energy of Christ. Our reversal of focus from ego to self and others illumines the cross, so that it is no longer seen as shadow but as light.

The cross demonstrates Jesus' overcoming entropy for us. God accepts the heaviness of the spiritual journey, and fills our emptiness. Christ redeems, buys back the lightness of the spiritual ascent for us so that we no longer must "swoon in the shadow of the cross, but may climb in the fire of its creative action."

It is
a terrifying thing to have been born:
I mean, to find oneself, without having willed it,
swept irrevocably along on a torrent of fearful energy
which seems as though it wished to destroy
everything it carries with it.

Plurality
(a residue of plurality
inseparable from all unification in progress)
is the most obvious source of our pain.
Externally it exposes us
to jars and makes us sensitive to these jars.
And internally it makes us fragile
and subject to countless kinds
 of physical disorders.
Everything
that has not "finished organizing"
must inevitably suffer from its residual lack
of organization and its possible disorganizations.
 Such is the human state.

The lines of the universe
do not bend back in closed curves
    within our being,
but are held together
as a sheaf within the unity of our ego
      only by their link with the future.
If the world were ripe in our souls,
we should find equilibrium and rest
    in our completion.
We should be able to be self-enclosed.
    Now the contrary is the case;
we are constantly escaping from ourselves
in our very effort to possess ourselves.

Once life has encroached so far,
only one reality (insofar as it truly exists)
     remains to confront it,
and can be compared to it in size and universality:
     this is entropy,
that mysterious involution
by which the world tends to progressively
     refurl on itself,
in unorganized plurality
and increasing probability,
the layer of cosmic energy.
And then, before our inquiring minds,
a final duel is fought
between life (thought) and entropy (matter)
     for the domination of the universe.

We avoid communication with another
because we are afraid that by sharing
    we will diminish our personalities.
We seek to grow by isolating ourselves.
Now if the universe is organically possible
(that is to say if it does not place us by birth
in a mechanically impossible position)
    the very opposite is true.
The gift we make of our being,
    far from threatening our ego,
        must have the effect of completing it.

Except in some exceptional cases
the "other" usually appears to be the worst danger
that our personality meets in the whole course
    of its development.
The other is a nuisance.
The other must be got out of the way.
The persons in the street get in my way
because I collide with them as possible rivals.
I shall like them
as soon as I see them as partners
    in the struggle.

Left to our own impulses
(but for the case of sexuality)
we would generally be much more susceptible
to mutual repulsion than to mutual attraction.
To be more ourselves, we try prematurely to be alone.
In opposition to this separatist instinct,
the necessities of life drive us into society.
Hence the manifold groupings,
which become ever more widespread and tyrannical,
whose tentacles multiply and seize us
    from all directions:
political, economic, religious associations.
Caught in these bonds, we have the impression
that our being is about to disappear;
       we go through the anguish of being choked.

Still lost in a crowd of our kind,
we turn away from a plurality which disturbs us.
　　We cannot love millions of strangers.
By revealing to each one
that a part of ourselves exists in all the rest,
the sense of the Earth is now bringing into sight
a new principle of universal affection
among the mass of living beings:
　　the devoted liking of one element for another
　　within a single world in progress.

Human units grow closer together,
not merely under the pressure of external forces
or solely by the performance of material acts,
        but directly,
center to center through internal attraction.
Not through coercion, or enslavement to a common task,
but through unanimity in a common spirit.

In order to unify in ourselves
or to unite with others,
we must change,
    renounce,
        give ourselves;
and this violence to ourselves partakes of pain.
Every advance in personalization must be paid for:
    so much union,
        so much suffering.

The evil in evil does not lie in the pain,
but in the feeling of diminishing through pain.
The greatest suffering you can think of will disappear,
    or even dissolve in a kind of pleasure,
provided you can discover a correlatively proportionate
achievement of which it has been the price.
Let us think what will be sufficient,
even in our unorganized state,
to compensate humanity for the anguish of its ills?
Simply for consciousness to awake to an object
        born from its sufferings.

The world is an immense groping,
　　an immense enterprise,
　　　　an immense attack;
its progress is made at the price of much failure
　　and many wounds.
The sufferers,
no matter to what species they belong,
are the expressions of this austere but noble condition.
They pay for the forward progress
　　and the victory of all.

What a vast ocean of human suffering
spreads over the entire Earth at every moment!
Of what is this mass formed?
Of blackness, gaps and rejections?
No, let me repeat, of potential energy.
In suffering, the ascending force of the world
        is concealed in a very intense form.
The whole question is how to liberate it
and give it a consciousness of its significance
and potentialities.
The world would leap high towards God
if all the sick together were to turn their pain into
a common desire that the kingdom of God
        should come to
rapid fruition through the conquest
and organization of the Earth.
May all the sufferers of the Earth
join their sufferings,
so that the world's pain
might become a great and unique act of consciousness,
        elevation,
            and union.

Do not brace yourself against suffering.
Try to close your eyes and surrender yourself,
    as if to a great loving energy.
This attitude is neither weak nor absurd,
it is the only one that cannot lead us astray.
Try to "sleep," with that *active* sleep of confidence
    which is that of the seed in the fields in winter.

When we feel that we are really alone in the world,
then (unless we tear one another to pieces)
we will begin to love one another.

We have become aware that,
in the great game that is being played,
we are the players as well as being the cards
     and the stakes. Nothing
can go on if we leave the table.
Neither can any power force us to remain.
Is the game worth the candle
or are we simply its dupes?
The last century
witnessed the first systematic strikes in industry;
the next will surely not pass
without the threat of strikes
     in the noosphere.

We waver today
between two desires:
to serve the world
or to go on strike.

Whether we become distorted,
　　disgusted,
　　　　or divided,
the result is equally bad
and certainly contrary
to that which Christianity should rightly produce
　　　　in us.

Judging by my own case, I would say
that the great temptation of this century is
(and will increasingly be)
that we find the World of nature,
of life, and of humankind greater,
closer,
more mysterious,
more alive,
than the God of Scripture.

I am afraid, too,
like all my fellow humans,
of the future too heavy with mystery
        and too wholly new,
towards which time is driving me.

How can it be
that "when I come down from the mountain"
and in spite of the glorious vision I still retain,
I find that I am so little better a person,
    so little at peace,
so incapable of expressing in my actions,
and thus adequately communicating to others,
        the wonderful unity that I feel encompassing me?

I begin to think that most of our weaknesses
are due to the fact that our "belief" is too narrow,
and that we don't believe through to the end.
To stop believing a second too soon,
or not to believe enough,
is sufficient to ruin the whole structure
    of what we are building.

What I want, my God,
is that by a reversal of focus
which you alone can bring about,
my terror in the face of nameless changes
    destined to renew my being
may be turned into an overflowing joy
at being transformed into you.

We must find a truly comprehensive formulation
of Christian renunciation;
without in any way
minimizing the doctrine of the Cross,
this must nevertheless integrate in Christian effort
all the dynamics contained in the lofty enthusiasms
of the human race.

Projected against a universe
where the struggle with evil is the condition
sine qua non of existence,
the Cross assumes new importance and fresh beauty,
and is capable of captivating us all the more.
Unquestionably Jesus is *still* he
who bears the sins of the world;
> in its own mysterious way
> suffering makes reparation for moral evil.

But above all
Jesus is he who overcomes structurally,
in himself and in behalf of us all,
that resistance to spiritual ascent
which is inherent in matter.
He is the One
who bears the weight which is inevitably part
    of all created reality.
He is both symbol of progress
and at the same time its heroic achievement.
The full and ultimate meaning of redemption
is no longer seen to be reparation alone,
    but rather further passage and conquest.

Christianity
does not ask us to live in the shadow of the Cross
but in the fire of its creative action.

3.

Union and Creativity

Introduction

Teilhard suggests that the plurality of our lives constantly appears as a demand for change or metamorphosis, and that this is experienced as suffering. We seek inner unity as a victory over this multiplicity, and logically expect to find it in isolation. However, we find that isolation cuts us off from the energy of the whole. If we move into the noosphere, then it is in union with all the rest that we must advance.

Union differentiates. The more energetically we are united with others, the more our creative differences bring the planet to higher development. This engagement of energies with others does not reduce our individuality. Rather, it enhances the creative consciousness and the discrete development of each person to full capacity.

The human species does not split and branch into separate forms as other species do, but folds in upon itself and forms one increasingly cohesive species. Teilhard calls this a process of "infolding" and calls this increasing cohesion "socialization" or "planetization." He considers this process to have two phases: one of expansion from the appearance of the human upon Earth until the mid-point of the Earth's development, and one of contraction from this mid-point until the ultimate development of the human spirit within Christ at the Omega Point is fulfilled.

During the long period of expansion, physical and cultural differences isolated the peoples of the Earth from each other as they spread to fill the Earth. At the beginning of our present century, with most of the habitable surface of the Earth occupied, the races began to converge. Through technology, tangential energy has created a complex organization of humanity. Radial energy becomes evident in the response of people across the Earth to each other; people are sharing their wars, their coronations, their concerns. Thus the law of complexity-consciousness develops.

Teilhard suggests that we are beginning this contraction phase in our generation, a period of evolution in which we will be more involved in psychological and spiritual relationships with all those who inhabit the planet. This will lead to the ultimate convergence—to the Omega Point.

Teilhard does not accept Darwin's "survival of the fittest" as applying to the human species. Though it is true for infra-human species, he insists that the opposite is true for the human. The human can progress only by converging, uniting. And this concept seems to him as revolutionary as the Copernican revolution or Darwinian evolution.

"Omega" is the last letter of the Greek alphabet, hence, the end of all. Teilhard uses it in two ways. At one time he applies it to the state of collective reflection achieved at the end of the process of evolution; and at other times he interprets it as a personal Being here and now responsible for the process.

This Omega which Teilhard sees as the Pleroma is the fusion of the cosmic with the Christic. At this point of convergence in space-time, the end of the Divine Milieu will come—the Parousia. Teilhard calls this Christogenesis, a synthesis of Christ with the universe.

This convergence becomes possible through love. Teilhard uses biological language when he speaks of the "phylum" (a bundle of cells of a particular species) and extrapolates the unities of this biological division as the "phylum of love" or law of amorization, his philosophy of love. Each person carries an energy aura. The convergence of these auras embraces the Earth within the noosphere. With love we unveil "the most powerful and unknown energy of the world."

Teilhard shares his revolutionary views of sexuality and marriage within his dynamic morality. In the 1930s he exhorts couples to liberate the energies of love. This requires not only the duties of procreating and educating children (the duties of the expansion phase of the planet) but also a serious commitment of the partners to their own spiritual growth as a couple (the duties of the convergent phase of the planet). Purity involves less sublimation and repression and more creative responsibility to savor and to love.

The incarnation event becomes the ultimate loving and creative process for Teilhard. The current of love surges from the person of the historic Christ, who *had* to enter into the process of physical evolution as an element in order to be the center of its convergence at the end point, Omega. As Christ inserts himself into time and space in our universe, all created matter becomes transformed and is incorporated into him. Teilhard, an early process theologian, insists that we complete Christ. As we struggle toward our own transformation, God also changes. God increases as the cosmic energy of love grows into true completion. And this is Christianity squared.

Nothing
is more beatific than union attained;
nothing more laborious than the pursuit of union.
For three reasons at least,
a personalizing evolution is necessarily painful:
it is basically a plurality;
it advances by differentiation;
it leads to metamorphoses.

Unity:
an abstract term, maybe,
in which philosophers delight;
and yet it is primarily a very concrete quality
with which we all dream of endowing our works
        and the world around us.
Happiness, power, wealth, wisdom, holiness:
these are all synonyms for a victory over the many.
At the heart of every being
lies the creation's dream of a principle which will one day
give organic form to its fragmented treasures.
        God is unity.

A person cannot disappear
by passing into another person;
for by nature we can only give ourselves as people
so long as we remain self-conscious units,
    that is to say distinct.
Moreover,
this gift which we make of ourselves
has the direct result of reinforcing
the most incommunicable quality,
that is to say
the quality of superpersonalizing.
    Union differentiates.

True union
does not fuse the elements it brings together,
by mutual fertilization and adaption it gives them
a renewal of vitality. It is egoism
that hardens and neutralizes the human stuff.
Union differentiates.

It is only toward hyper-reflection—
that is to say, hyper-personalization—
        that thought can extrapolate itself.
It is a mistake to look for the extension
of our being or of the noosphere in the impersonal.
In any domain—whether it be
the cells of the body, the members of a soceity
or the elements of a spiritual synthesis—
        union differentiates.
In every organized whole,
the parts perfect themselves and fulfill themselves.
It is a mistake
to confuse individuality with personality.
To be fully ourselves
it is in the direction of convergence
with all the rest that we must advance—
        toward the "other."
The peak of ourselves,
the acme of our originality,
is not our individuality but our person;
and according to
the evolutionary structure of the world,
we can only find our person by uniting together.
Socialization means not the end but rather
        the beginning of the Era of Person.

Let us
advance one step further.
What name should we give
to this physio-moral energy of personalization
to which all activities displayed by the stuff
of the universe are finally reduced?
Only one name is possible,
if we are to credit it with the generality and power
that it should assume on rising
    to the cosmic order:
        love.

The conclusion
is always the same:
love is the most powerful
and still the most unknown energy
of the world.

From the critical moment of hominization,
another more essential role was developed for love,
a role of which
we are seemingly only just beginning
    to feel the importance;
I mean the necessary synthesis
of the two principles,
    male and female,
        in the building of the human personality.

Here the cosmic role
of sexuality appears in its full breadth.
And here at the same time, the rules appear which
will guide us in the mastery of
that terrifying energy in which
the power that causes
the universe to converge on itself
        passes through us.
The first of these rules is that love,
in conformity with the general laws of creative union,
contributes to the spiritual differentiations
of the two beings which it brings together.
        The one must not absorb the other
nor, still less, should the two lose themselves
in the enjoyments of physical possession,
which would signify
a lapse into plurality and return to nothingness.
    Love is an adventure
and a conquest.
It survives
and develops like the universe itself
        only by perpetual discovery.

Little by little,
love becomes distinct,
though still *confused* for a very long time
with the simple function of reproduction.
No longer only a unique and periodic attraction
for purposes of material fertility;
but an unbounded and continuous possibility
of contact between minds rather than bodies;
the play of countless subtle antennae
seeking one another in the light
    and darkness of the soul;
        the pull towards
            mutual sensibility and completion.

When the maturing of its personality
is approaching for the Earth,
humans will have to realize that it is for them
    not simply a question of controlling births,
but of increasing to the utmost
the quantity of love liberated
    from the duty of reproduction.
Enforced by this new need,
the essentially personalizing function of love
will detach itself more or less completely
from "the flesh" which has been for a time
    the organ of propagation.
Without ceasing to be physical,
    in order to remain physical,
        love will make itself more spiritual.

Man and woman
    for the child,
        still and for so long
as life on Earth has not reached maturity.
But man and woman for one another
    increasingly and for ever.

Because the world
   is always growing
     and always unfinished
     and always ahead of us,
to achieve our love we are engaged in
a limitless conquest of the universe and ourselves.
In this sense, we can only attain each other
by consummating a union with the universe.
Love is a sacred reserve of energy;
   it is like the blood
     of spiritual evolution.

Energy, then, becomes Presence.
And so the possibility
is disclosed for,
opens out for,
humanity,
not only of believing and hoping but
(what is much more unexpected and
    much more valuable)
        of loving.
Co-existing
and co-organically with all the past,
the present and the future of the Universe
    is in a process
        of concentration upon itself.

Purity
simply denotes the more-or-less distinct manner
in which the ultimate centre of their coincidence
    appears above the two beings in love.
No question here of leaving one another,
but only of joining in a greater than themselves.
The world
does not become divine by suppression
    but by sublimation.
Its sanctity is not an elimination
    but a concentration of the sap of the Earth.

To love
is to discover and complete one's self
in someone other than oneself,
an act impossible of general realization on Earth
so long as each can see in the neighbor no more than
a closed fragment following its own course
            through the world.
It is precisely
this state of isolation that will end
if we begin to discover in each other
not merely the elements of one and the same thing,
but of a single Spirit in search of itself.
The existence of such a power
becomes possible in the curvature of a world
            capable of noogenesis.

Nothing is precious
except that part of you which is in other people
and that part of others which is in you.
 Up there,
   on high,
     everything is one.

Love
is the free and imaginative outflowing
of the Spirit over all unexplored paths.
It links those
who love in bonds that unite,
but do not destroy,
causing them to discover in their mutual contact
an exaltation capable of stirring in the very core
of their being all that they possess
of "uniqueness" and "creative" power.
Love alone
can unite living beings
so as to complete and fulfill them,
for it alone joins them by what is deepest
in themselves. All we need
is to imagine our ability to love
developing until it embraces the totality
of the people of the Earth.

A universal love
is not only psychologically possible;
it is the only complete and final way
in which we are able to love.

There is,
in truth, a secret message,
explanatory of the whole of Creation,
which by allowing us to feel God in everything we do
and in everything that is done to us
(God creating in all things
and being born in all things)
    can bring true happiness
        to our generation.
Christ is incarnate;
incarnate through the combined action
of determinant and liberating factors,
        and of grace.

There are *two sides* to this operation,
    the *constructive* and the *destructive*;
and when Christ is installed at Omega Point
    it is both these two sides that are covered
        and permeated by a flood of unitive force.
In one great surge,
Cosmogenesis becomes personalized,
    both in the things it adds,
    which *centrify us for Christ*,
        and in the things it subtracts,
which draw us out of our own centers onto him.
A current of love is all at once released,
to spread over the whole breadth
    and depth of the World:
        and this it does as a fundamental essence
which will metamorphose all things,
    assimilate
        and take the place of all.

The more I reflect
upon the profound laws of evolution,
the more I am convinced that the Universal Christ
would be unable to appear at the end of time
    at the world's summit,
unless
he had previously inserted himself
into the course of the world's movement
    by way of birth in the form of an element.

There is nothing strange
about there being a physical element in Christ.
Each one of us, if we but reflect,
    is enveloped,
        aureoled by an extension of being
            as vast as the universe.
What we are aware
of is only the nucleus which is ourselves.
The interaction of souls would be incomprehensible
if some "aura" did not extend from one to the other,
something proper to each one
    and common to all.

Starting from an evolutive Omega
at which we assume Christ to stand,
not only does it become possible
to conceive Christ as radiating *physically*
over the terrifying totality of things,
but, what is more,
that radiation must inevitably work up to
    a maximum of penetrative and activating power.
        The cosmic-Christ
            becomes cosmically possible.
To sum up,
Cosmogenesis reveals itself,
along the line of its main axis,
    first as Biogenesis
        and then Noogenesis,
            and finally culminates in the Christogenesis.

The presence of the Incarnate Word
penetrates like a universal element.
It shines at the heart of all things.

Not in a metaphysical but in a *physical* sense,
the Energy of Incarnation was to flow into,
and so illuminate and give warmth to,
ever wider and more tightly
    encircling forms of embrace.

By virtue of the Creation
and, still more, of the Incarnation,
nothing here below is *profane* for those
who know how to see.

Christ does not act
as a dead or passive point of convergence,
but as a center of radiation for the energies
that lead the universe back to God through humanity,
the layers of divine action finally come to us
impregnated with divine organic energies.

Christ is seen
in the extension of the human ideal—
and the God of the Christians emerges
as identical with the deity
of whom the Earth dreams:
    as great,
        as immediate,
            as concerned in our progress,
            as the Universe.

As a direct consequence
of the unitive process by which God is revealed to us,
God in some way "transforms self"
  when incorporating us.
So, it is no longer a matter of simply seeing God
and allowing oneself to be enveloped
and penetrated by God—
  we have to do more:
    we have to disclose God
(or even in one sense of the word "complete" God)
ever more fully.
  All around us,
    and within our own selves,
      God is in process of "changing"
as a result of the coincidence of God's magnetic power
    and our own Thought.
As the "Quantity of cosmic Union" rises,
so the brilliance increases
  and the glow
    of God's coloring
      grows richer.

God can in the future
be experienced and apprehended
(and can even, in a true sense, be completed)
by the whole ambient totality
    of what we call Evolution.
This is still,
of course, Christianity
and always will be,
but a Christianity reincarnated
    for the second time
(Christianity, we might say, squared)
    in the spiritual energies of Matter.

4.

Compassion and Celebration

Introduction

If we accept the union of all creation with God as the basic common goal, we incur a moral relationship to all persons, for the age of nations is past. No nation owns the air, the water, the fire energy of the Earth. Ownership of the Earth takes on a new meaning in this age of convergence.

In 1937, Teilhard created a new dynamic morality to replace the static morality based on Roman law. Static morality protects individual property and the autonomy of each society. This maintains a static equilibrium which limits energy forces. As we live in an evolving universe, the problem is not to protect the possessions of the individual so much as to guide the person to wholeness, in order that the spiritual energies of the planet may reach their highest development.

In a dynamic morality, life and personal gifts must be used in the service of the cosmos; the possession of wealth must work in the direction of the spirit; and the marriage unity is embraced for the complementary spiritual development of the partners. The "best" in this dynamic morality is whatever assures the highest development of complexity-consciousness within the spiritual powers of the Earth. "For life is groping, adventurous, and dangerous."

Teilhard defines religion as the long disclosure of God's Being within the human experience. This pattern of disclosure initiated by God persuades us out of our isolation and moves us toward union with all creation. Teilhard struggled with organized "religion" from his youth. He could not accept the institutional nega-tion of matter, and the assumption that God was found *above* mat-ter. For Teilhard the horizontal flow of relationship with the Earth and with others (the forward thrust) was as important as the verti-cal relationship to God. He is eager to direct us to the God ahead, as well as to the God above. But he agrees that it is the function of religion to direct our psychic energy toward our spiritual search.

Teilhard suffered intensely because the Roman Catholic hier-archy determined that he should not teach or publish his writings. Ironically, his deep belief and trust in evolution kept him locked into this tradition. To leave the church would have put him outside the evolution of tradition, and he realized the slowness of evolu-tion. He tells us that the "theological encrustations" are tolerable for him, for Christ remains within the church as the Sun/Son.

Because of his very tentative status with the authorities, Teil-hard seldom wrote about Eastern philosophies, though he was interested in them, and he critiques pantheism upon occasion. He suggests that the early pantheistic philosophies teach of a world that is permeated by creative love. But it is Christianity that binds the Cosmic, the Human, and the Christic into a unity—the Centric.

In 1933, he speaks against the prevalent understanding of religion as predominantly personal sacrifice. He exhorts us to adoration of God through our creativity—giving ourselves to that forward movement through creative intellectual exploration. This is the purest form of charity, and the new form of mysticism. With our efforts and energies we complete the world, we bring fulfill-ment to God, and we move the universe closer to the Omega Point.

And this calls for celebration. We find our celebration through the Eucharist. For Teilhard, the Eucharist includes the Earth—the Earth of our origins consecrated through our labors, joys, and sufferings. The planet is the immense host. The ritual becomes our search.

And a fresh kind of life begins.

Morality
has hitherto been individualistic
(the relation of individuals to individuals).
In the future
more explicit emphasis will have to be laid
on our obligations to collective bodies
and even to the Universe:
on political duties,
social duties,
international duties,
on cosmic duties,
first among which stands the Law of Work and Research.

The powers
that we have released,
could not possibly be absorbed
by the narrow system of individual or national units
which the architects of the human Earth
	have hitherto used.
The age of nations has passed.
Now, unless we wish to perish
	we must shake off our old prejudices
		and build the Earth.

Religion
is not a strictly individual crisis—
      or choice
            or intuition—
but represents the long disclosure of God's being
through the collective experience of the whole
      of humanity. . .
God bent over
the now intelligent mirror of Earth
to impress on it the first marks of beauty.

The conflict
is not between Christianity and atheism,
but between the old and traditional faith
    in a celestial escape *upward*
and another new faith,
in an evolutionary escape *forward*;
and the capital thing to see
is that between *upward* and *forward*
    there is no contradiction
        but essential complementarity.

You know that for some time now the principal interest
    in my life is no longer Fossil Human,
but the Human of tomorrow;
or, more exactly, "the God of tomorrow,"
since I am more and more convinced that the great event
of our time
    is a kind of change in the face of God
in which the pure "God of above" of yesterday
        is beng combined
            with a kind of "God of ahead"
(in extension of the Human).

More and more
I see growing in me
the evidence and the human consequences
of the great thing that is happening right now.
Not "God who is dying," as Nietzsche said,
 but "God who is changing,"
so that,
as I am in the habit of saying,
the Upward movement is now reinforced
by a Forward movement never before considered
 by the religions.

I am extremely sensitive
to the excess of complication
and specialization that encumbers
present-day religious confession. Owing to atavism
and education, no doubt,
        but also to reason,
I seem to perceive in the parasitic network
an inevitable biological phenomenon which requires
        and foretells a sloughing-off.
            I admit all the defects,
but I tolerate them even as I react against them,
because for now they are inseparable
from what seems to be the only axis
along which human activity can legitimately progress.
Believe me,
when one has penetrated
to this axis of the Christian attitude,
the ritual,
disciplinary and theological encrustations
matter little more than musical or acoustical theories
matter to the enjoyment
        of a beautiful
            piece of music.

Christ is in the Church
in the same way as the sun
is before our eyes.
We see the same sun as our fathers saw,
and yet we understand it
in a much more magnificent way.

I realize more clearly
that my possibilities and tendencies
are not exactly to start any definite social movement,
but to help to create a kind of spiritual atmosphere
in which the whole of each life should be
   enlightened, transformed,
just as a precious stone
by a ray of the proper light
creates the feeling that the whole world is permeated
   by a creative love.
This is, of course,
essentially the Christian attitude,
but made richer by a confluence with the best
and subtle essence of what is hidden
   behind the various pantheisms.

To *extend* the kingdom of God
to new peoples is well enough.
But it is still better,
    and more direct,
        to *make it penetrate*
into the deep rooted "thrust"
in which Humankind's desires are today combining.

Here we move into what is indeed a remarkable,
an astonishing region where the Cosmic,
the Human and the Christic meet
and so open up a new domain,
        the *Centric*;
                and there the manifold oppositions
which constitute the unhappiness
and anxieties of our life
        begin to disappear.

Up until now,
to adore has meant
to prefer God to things by referring them to God
and by sacrificing them to God.
Now adoration means
the giving of our body and soul to creative activity,
joining that activity to God
to bring the world to fulfillment
by effort
and intellectual exploration.

Do not forget that the value and interest of life
is not so much to do conspicuous things
(although we must have this ambition)
as to do ordinary things
with the perception of their enormous value.
This, I think, is the mystic to come.

We are all of us together
carried in the one world-womb;
yet each of us is our own little microcosm
in which the Incarnation is wrought independently
with degrees of intensity
and shades that are incommunicable.

There is the evidence
provided by the *contagious power*
        of a form of Charity
in which it becomes possible to love God
"not only with all one's body and all one's soul"
        but with the whole Universe-in-Evolution.

Theoretically,
this transformation of love is quite possible.
What paralyzes life is failure to believe
        and failure to dare.
The day will come when,
after harnessing space,
        the winds,
            the tides,
                and gravitation,
we shall harness for God the energies of love.
And, on that day, for the second time
in the history of the world,
        we shall have discovered fire.

Thus we must *build*—
starting with the most natural territory
of our own self—a work,
    an *opus*,
into which something enters
from all the elements of the Earth.
We make our own souls
throughout all our earthly days;
and at the same time we collaborate in another work,
    another *opus*,
which infinitely transcends,
while at the same time it narrowly determines,
the perspectives of our individual achievements:
      The completing of the World.
That is, ultimately,
the meaning and value of our acts.
Owing to the interrelation between matter,
     Soul and Christ,
we bring part of the being which he desires
back to God *in whatever we do.*
With each of our works
we labor in individual separation
but no less really to build the Pleroma;
that is to say we bring to Christ
    a little fulfillment.

These perspectives
will appear absurd to those
who don't see that life is,
from its origins,
groping,
    adventurous,
        and dangerous.
But these perspectives will grow,
like an irresistible idea on the horizon
        of new generations.

It is
first by the Incarnation
and next by the Eucharist
that Christ organizes us for himself
and imposes himself upon us.
By his Incarnation
he inserted himself not just into humanity
    but into the universe which supports humanity.

It seems to me that in a sense
the true substance to be consecrated each day
is the world's development during that day—
        the bread
symbolizing appropriately
what creation succeeds in producing,
        the wine (blood)
what creation causes to be lost
in exhaustion and suffering
    in the course of its effort.

I will make the whole Earth my altar
and on it will offer You all the labors
and sufferings of the world.

Over every living
thing which is to spring up,
    to grow,
        to flower,
            to ripen during this day,
say again the words: This is my Body.
And over every death-force
which awaits in readiness to corrode,
    to wither,
        to cut down,
speak again your commanding words
which express the supreme mystery of faith:
        This is my Blood.

In the humanity
which is begotten today,
the Word prolongs the unending act
    of God's own birth;
and by virtue
of God's immersion in the world's womb,
the great waters of the kingdom of matter have,
without even a ripple, been embued with life.
    The Immense host
        which is the universe
           is made flesh.

For you, there is only one road
that can lead to God and this is fidelity
to remain constantly true to yourself,
to what you feel is highest in you.
The road will open before you as you go.

Just trust Life:
Life will bring you high,
if only you are careful in selecting,
in the maze of events, those influences or those paths
which can bring you each time
    a little more upward.
Life has to be discovered
    and built step by step:
        a great charm,
if only one is convinced
(by faith and experience)
    that the world is going somewhere.

The future
is more beautiful
than all the pasts.

A fresh kind of life
is starting.

§

Acknowledgments

Acknowledgment is given to the following publishers for permission to reprint selections from their works:

Excerpts from *The Future of Man, The Divine Milieu, Letters from a Traveler, Hymn of the Universe,* and *The Phenomenon of Man* by Teilhard de Chardin, and *The Life of Teilhard de Chardin* by Robert Speaight, copyright © 1969, 1960, 1968, 1965, 1959, 1967 respectively by Harper & Row, Publishers, Inc., are reprinted by permission of Harper & Row, Publishers, Inc., New York, New York.

Excerpts from *The Heart of Matter, Human Energy, Christianity and Evolution,* and *Toward the Future,* by Teilhard de Chardin, copyright © 1976, 1973, 1969, 1962 respectively by Editions du Seuil, English translation copyright © 1978, 1975, 1971, 1969 respectively by William Collins Sons & Co. Ltd. and Harcourt Brace Jovanovich, Inc., are reprinted by permission of Harcourt Brace Jovanovich, Inc., Orlando, Florida.

Excerpts from *Building the Earth* by Teilhard de Chardin, copyright © 1965 by Dimension Books, are reprinted by permission of Dimension Books, Denville, New Jersey.

Excerpts from *Writings in Time of War,* originally published in the U.S. by Harper & Row Publishers, Inc., New York, New York, © 1968, are used with the permission of the literary executor for the estate of Teilhard de Chardin and Editions Bernard Grasset, in care of Georges Borchardt, Inc. literary agency, New York.

References

All books cited are by Pierre Teilhard de Chardin, unless otherwise noted. All of his work was published posthumously in several collections of essays; the dates of the essays themselves vary considerably within each book.

This reference section lists the page of this book on which each quotation is found, and the source from which it was obtained. The source listing contains an abbreviation of the source title (as recorded in the directory below), the name of the essay referenced, the date on which the essay was originally written, and the page number from the source. Dates given for whole source books are the dates on which these books were originally written by Teilhard.

Books by Pierre Teilhard de Chardin:

BE: *Building the Earth*. Wilkes-Barre, PA: Dimensions Books, 1965.

CE: *Christianity and Evolution*. New York: Harcourt Brace Jovanovich, 1971.

DM: *The Divine Milieu*. New York: Harper & Row, 1960.

FM: *The Future of Man*. New York: Harper & Row, 1969.

HM: *The Heart of Matter*. New York: Harcourt Brace Jovanovich, 1978.

HE: *Human Energy*. New York: Harcourt Brace Jovanovich, 1978.

HU: *Hymn of the Universe*. New York: Harper & Row, 1965.

LT: *Letters from a Traveler*. New York: Harper & Row, 1968.

LTF: *Letters to Two Friends 1926-1952*. New York: New American Library, 1968.

PM: *The Phenomenon of Man*. New York: Harper & Row, 1959.

PU: *The Prayer of the Universe*. New York: Harper & Row, 1973.

TF: *Toward the Future*. New York: Harcourt Brace Jovanovich, 1975.

WTW: *Writings in Time of War*. New York: Harper & Row, 1968.

Books about Pierre Teilhard de Chardin:

TCW: Faricy, Robert. *Teilhard de Chardin's Theology of the Christian in the World*. New York: Sheed and Ward, 1967.

TCMC: Mooney, Christopher. *Teilhard de Chardin and the Mystery of Christ*. Garden City, N.Y.: Doubleday, 1968.

LTC: Speaight, Robert. *The Life of Teilhard de Chardin*. New York: Harper & Row, 1967.

References for Chapter 1: ORIGINS

PAGE	SOURCE	
20	HM:	from "Heart of Matter' (1950) p. 71.
21	HU:	from "Mass on the World" (1923) p. 21.
22	HM:	from "Heart of Matter" (1950) p. 85.
23	PM:	(1938) p. 78.
24	HU:	from "Mass on the World" (1923) p. 22.
25	HM:	from "Heart of Matter" (1950) p. 25.
26	HE:	from "Spirit of Earth" (1931) p. 41.
27	PU:	from "Mystical Milieu" (1917) p. 124.
28	HM:	from "Heart of Matter" (1950) p. 33.
29	PM:	(1938) p. 221.
30	HM:	from "Heart of Matter" (1950) p. 35.
31	PU:	from "Mystical Milieu" (1917) p. 124.
32	HE:	from "Sketch of a Personalistic Universe" (1936) p. 82.
33	BE:	(1931) p. 117.
34	HM:	from "Heart of Matter" (1950) p. 28.
35	HM:	from "Heart of Matter" (1950) p. 26-7.
36	HM:	from "Heart of Matter" (1950) p. 50.
37	HM:	from "My Intellectual Position" (1948) p. 143.
38	HM:	from "Heart of Matter" (1950) p. 36.

PAGE	SOURCE	
39	HM:	from "Heart of Matter" (1950) p. 32.
40	PM:	(1938) p. 251-2.
41	HM:	from "Heart of Matter" (1950) p. 37.
42	HM:	from "The Christic" (1955) p. 86.
43	WTW:	from "Forma Christi" (1918) p. 262.
44	HM:	from "Note on the Presentation of the Gospel" (1919) p. 222.
45	HM:	from "The Christic" (1955) p. 96-7.
46	LTC:	(from letter written in 1920) p. 109.
47	HM:	from "Heart of Matter" (1950) p. 71.
48	HM:	from "The Christic" (1955) p. 101.

References for Chapter 2: EMPTYING

PAGE	SOURCE	
52	HU:	from "Mass on the World" (1923) p. 29.
53	HE:	from "Sketch of a Personalistic Universe" (1936) p. 85.
54	HE:	from "Sketch of a Personalistic Universe" (1936) p. 62.
55	HE:	from "Spirit of Earth " (1931) p. 22.
56	HE:	from "Sketch of a Personalistic Universe" (1936) p. 63.
57	HE:	from "Sketch of a Personalistic Universe" (1936) p. 78.
58	HE:	from "Sketch of a Personalistic Universe" (1936) pp. 64.
59	HE:	from "Spirit of Earth" (1931) p. 35.
60	FM:	from "Life and the Planets" (1946) p. 123.
61	HE:	from "Sketch of a Personalistic Universe" (1936) p. 87.
62	HE:	from "Sketch of a Personalistic Universe" (1936) p. 88.

PAGE	SOURCE	
63	HE:	from "The Significance and Positive Value of Suffering" (1933) p. 50.
64	HE:	from "The Significance and Positive Value of Suffering" (1933) p. 51.
65	LTF:	(1948) p. 104.
66	HM:	from 'The Great Monad" (1918) p. 188.
67	PM:	(1938) p. 230.
68	HE:	from "Spirit of Earth" (1933) p. 44.
69	DM:	(1927) p. 52.
70	HM:	from "My Universe" (1918) p. 207.
71	HU:	from "Mass on the World" (1923) p. 30.
72	HM:	from "The Christic" (1955) p. 100.
73	LTC:	from "Letter to Zanta" (1929) p. 174.
74	HU:	from "Mass on the World" (1923) p. 29.
75	HM:	from "Note on the Presentation of the Gospel" (1919) p. 220.
76	FM:	from "The New Spirit" (1946) p. 89.
77	FM:	from "The New Spirit" (1946) p. 89.
78	DM:	(1927) p. 104.

References for Chapter 3: UNION AND CREATIVITY

PAGE	SOURCE	
83	HE:	from "Sketch of a Personalistic Universe" (1936) p. 85.
84	HM:	from "Two Wedding Addresses" (1935) p. 140.
85	HE:	from "Sketch of a Personalistic Universe" (1936) p. 67.
86	HE:	from "Sketch of a Personalistic Universe" (1936) p. 63.
87	PM:	(1938) p. 259-63.
88	HE:	from "Sketch of a Personalistic Universe" (1936) p. 72.
89	LTF:	(letter written in 1948) p. 182.

PAGE	SOURCE	
90	HE:	from "Sketch of a Personalistic Universe" (1936) p. 73.
91	HE:	from "Sketch of a Personalistic Universe" (1936) p. 74.
92	HE:	from "Spirit of Earth" (1931) p. 33.
93	HE:	from "Sketch of a Personalistic Universe" (1936) p. 77.
94	HE:	from "Sketch of a Personalistic Universe" (1936) p. 73.
95	HE:	from "Spirit of Earth" (1931) p. 34.
96	HM:	from "The Christic" (1955) p. 99.
97	HE:	from "Sketch of a Personalistic Universe" (1936) p. 76.
98	FM:	from "The New Spirit" (1942) p. 95.
99	LTC:	(letter written in 1920) p. 109.
100	FM:	from "The Grand Option" (1939) p. 57.
101	PM:	(1938) p. 267.
102	HM:	from "Note on the Presentation of the Gospel" (1919) p. 216.
103	HM:	from "Heart of Matter" (1950) p. 51.
104	TCMC:	p. 81.
105	WTW:	from "Forma Christi" (1918) p. 253.
106	HM:	from "The Christic" (1955) p. 94.
107	TCW:	p. 119.
108	HE:	from "Heart of Matter" (1919) p. 48.
109	DM:	(1927) p. 66.
110	DM:	(1927) p. 123.
111	HM:	from "Note on the Presentation of the Gospel" (1919) p. 216.
112	HM:	from "Heart of Matter" (1919) p. 53.
113	HM:	from "The Christic" (1955) p. 96.

References for Chapter 4: COMPASSION AND CELEBRATION

PAGE	SOURCE	
118	HM:	from "Note on the Presentation of the Gospel" (1919) p. 220.

PAGE	SOURCE	
119	HE:	from "Spirit of Earth" (1931) p. 37.
120	HE:	from "Spirit of Earth" (1931) p. 47.
121	LTF:	(letter written in 1948) p. 186.
122	LTF:	(1950) p. 114.
123	LTF:	(1950) p. 113.
124	LTF:	(1926) p. 30.
125	HM:	from "On my Attitude to the Official Church" (1921) p. 117.
126	LTF:	(1939) p. 128.
127	HM:	from "Note on the Presentation of the Gospel" (1919) p. 221.
128	HM:	from "Heart of Matter" (1950) p. 49.
129	CE:	from "Christianity and Evolution" (1933) p. 92.
130	LTF:	(1941) p. 156.
131	HU:	from "The Mass on the World" (1923) p. 28.
132	HM:	from "The Christic" (1950) p. 101.
133	TF:	from "The Evolution of Chastity" (1934) p. 86.
134	DM:	(1927) p. 61-62.
135	HE:	from "The Phenomenon of Spirituality" (1937) p. 108.
136	WTW:	from "Cosmic Life" (1916) p. 51.
137	LT:	(1923) p. 86.
138	HU:	from "Mass on the World" (1923) p. 19.
139	HU:	from "Mass on the World" (1923) p. 23.
140	HU:	from "Mass on the World" (1923) p. 24.
141	LTF:	(1926) p. 31.
142	LTF:	(1939) p. 127.
143	LTC:	p. 110.
144	BE:	from "We Must Save the Earth" (1937) p. 19.

To receive information about a videotape, cards, and paintings on Teilhard themes, please write to Sr. Blanche Marie Gallagher, B.V.M., at Mundelein College, 6363 N. Sheridan Road, Chicago, IL. 60660.

Books of Related Interest
by Bear & Company

THE BOOK OF ANGELUS SILESIUS
With Observations by the Ancient Zen Masters
by Frederick Franck

EARTH ASCENDING
An Illustrated Treatise on the Law Governing Whole Systems
by José Argüelles

FIREBALL AND THE LOTUS
Emerging Spirituality from Ancient Roots
edited by Ron Miller & Jim Kenney

ORIGINAL BLESSING
A Primer in Creation Spirituality
by Matthew Fox

TO CARE FOR THE EARTH
A Call to a New Theology
by Sean McDonagh

THE UNIVERSE IS A GREEN DRAGON
A Cosmic Creation Story
by Brian Swimme

WESTERN SPIRITUALITY
Historical Roots, Ecumenical Routes
edited by Matthew Fox

Contact your local bookseller or write:
BEAR & COMPANY
P.O. Drawer 2860
Santa Fe, NM 87504